# *The Little Gardener's* COOKBOOK

## A child's guide to gardening and cooking

WRITTEN AND ILLUSTRATED
BY KATHLEEN BULLOCK

## THE BEST SELLERS PUBLISHING COMPANY

*For Walter, the*
*Master Gardener*

Copyright© 1986 by The Best Sellers Publishing Co.
All rights reserved.
Printed and bound in the United States.
Library of Congress Cataloging in Publication Data.
ISBN 0-937545-02-3
First Edition
Second Printing, December 1987

Published by:

The Best Sellers Publishing Co.

This Gardening-Cook Book
is presented with Love and Affection

to _____

on _____
                    date

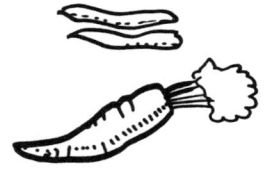

by _____

_____

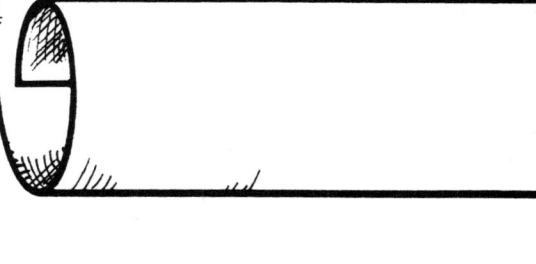

Happy Gardening and Good Cooking!

# MORE "BEST SELLERS" BOOKS AND GIFTS

STARVING STUDENTS COOKBOOK . . . . . . . . . . . . . . . . . . . . . . . . . . . .$7.95
STARVING STUDENTS SURVIVAL KIT. . . . . . . . . . . . . . . . . . . . .$18.95
LITTLE GARDNER'S COOKBOOK. . . . . . . . . . . . . . . . . . . . . . . . . . .$7.95
     Ages 5 – 10
LITTLE GARDNER'S GROW AND COOK KIT . . . . . . . . . . . . . . .$17.95
KID'S WEEKLY PLANNER . . . . . . . . . . . . . . . . . . . . . . . . . . . . . . . .$9.95
     (for Home – for School)
WHO IS THAT SHORT CHEF? . . . . . . . . . . . . . . . . . . . . . . . . . . . . .$7.95
     Ages 6 – 12
I'M A SHORT CHEF APRON . . . . . . . . . . . . . . . . . . . . . . . . . . . . . .$10.00
COFFEE FOR EVERY OCCASION . . . . . . . . . . . . . . . . . . . . . . . . .$10.00
     Includes 4 coffee coasters
FOWL PLAY (A Chicken Lovers Cookbook) . . . . . . . . . . . . . . . . . .$7.95

Price includes handling and shipping (California residents add 6½% tax)

## ORDER FROM:

**The Best Sellers Publishing Co.**
**9300 Gardenia Avenue**
**Fountain Valley, CA 92708**
**(714) 968-9102**
**1-(800)-227-6420**

NOTE: AS A SPECIAL ADDED FEATURE. . . . .

If you wish these delightful books sent as a gift, please include any greetings you may want and complete shipping address.

# CONTENTS

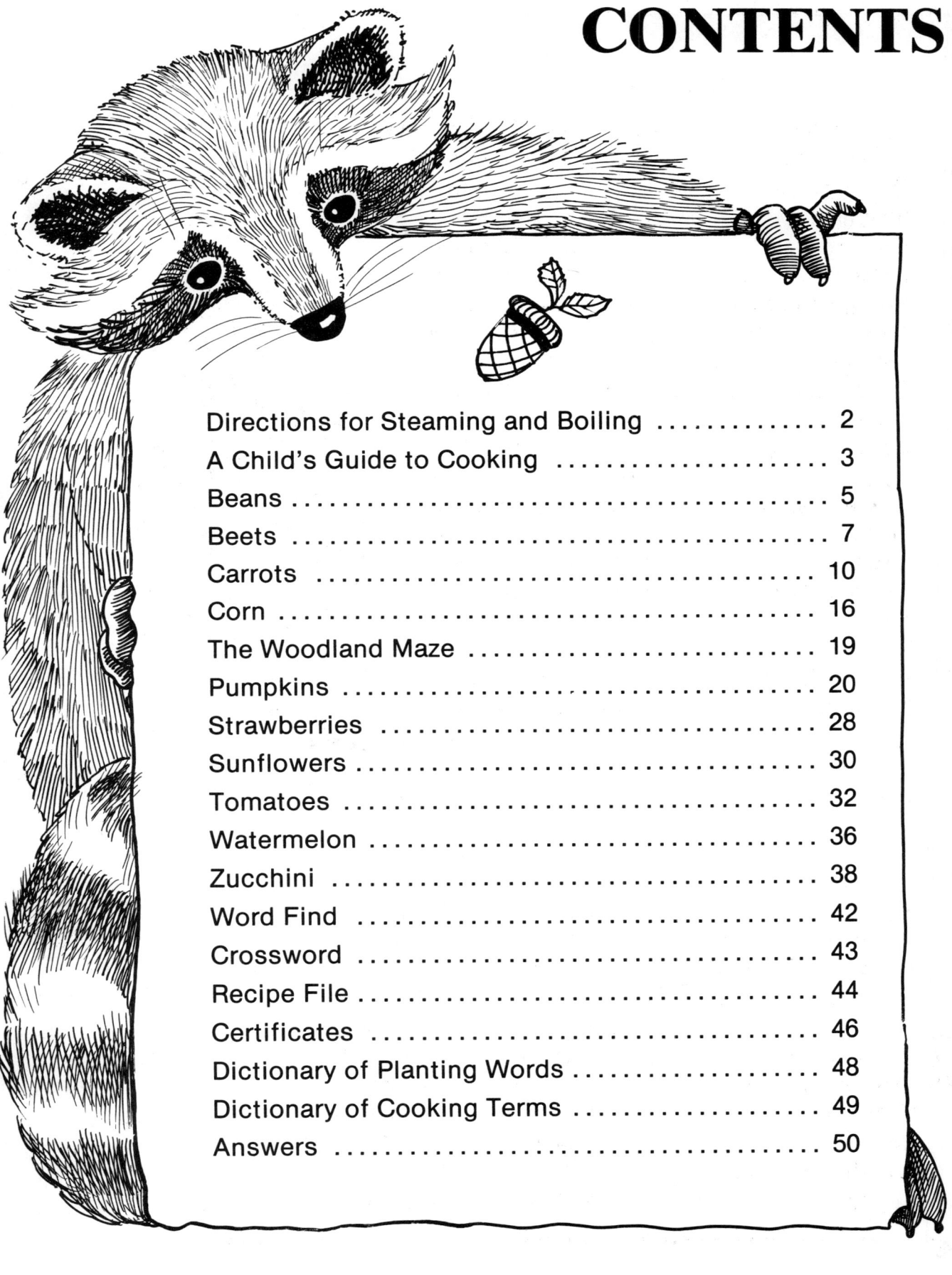

## STEAMING

| | |
|---|---|
| Artichokes . . . . . . . . . . . . . | 40–45 mins. |
| Asparagus . . . . . . . . . . . . . | 20–25 mins. |
| Green beans . . . . . . . . . . . | 15 mins. |
| Beet greens . . . . . . . . . . . . | 5–7 mins. |
| Beets . . . . . . . . . . . . . | 20–30 mins. |
| Broccoli . . . . . . . . . . . | 15–20 mins. |
| Brussels Sprouts . . . . . . . . . | 15–20 mins. |
| Cabbage . . . . . . . . . . . . | 25 mins. |
| Carrots . . . . . . . . . . . . . . | 10–15 mins. |
| Cauliflower . . . . . . . . . . . . | 10 mins. |
| Celery . . . . . . . . . . . | Not usually steamed |
| Corn . . . . . . . . . . . . . . . . . | 10 mins. |
| Eggplant . . . . . . . . . | Not usually steamed |
| Onions, whole . . . . . . . . . . | 10–15 mins. |
| Peas . . . . . . . . . . . . . . . . | 10 mins. |
| Potatoes . . . . . . . . . | Not usually steamed |
| Sweet potatoes . . . . | Not usually steamed |
| Spinach . . . . . . . . . . . . . | 5–7 mins. |
| Summer squash . . . . . . . . . | 5–10 mins. |
| Winter squash . . . . . . . . . . | 10–15 mins. |
| Tomatoes . . . . . . . . | Not usually steamed |
| Turnips . . . . . . . . . . . . . . . . | 10–15 mins. |

## BOILING

| | | | |
|---|---|---|---|
| Artichokes . . . . . . . . . . | 20–30 min. | Corn . . . . . . . . . . . | 7–12 min. |
| Asparagus . . . . . . . . . . . | 10–20 min. | Eggplant . . . . . . . . . . . . | 6–10 min. |
| Beans, shell or string . . . . | 15–20 min. | Onions . . . . . . . . . . . . . | 15–45 min. |
| Beet greens . . . . . . . . . . | 8–12 min. | Peas . . . . . . . . . . . . . . . | 12–15 min. |
| Beets . . . . . . . . . . . . . | 20–45 min. | Potatoes . . . . . . . . . . . . | 20–45 min. |
| Broccoli . . . . . . . . . . . | 12–15 min. | Sweet Potatoes . . . . . . . | 25–30 min. |
| Brussels sprouts . . . . . . . | 15–20 min. | Spinach . . . . . . . . . . . . | 8–12 min. |
| Cabbage . . . . . . . . . . . | 8–12 min. | Summer Squash . . . . . . . | 12–20 min. |
| Carrots . . . . . . . . . . . . | 15–30 min. | Winter Squash . . . . . . . | 45–60 min. |
| Cauliflower . . . . . . . . . . | 15–25 min. | Tomatoes . . . . . . . . . . . | 10–12 min. |
| Celery . . . . . . . . . . . . | 10–25 min. | Turnips . . . . . . . . . . . . | 12–20 min. |

# a child's guide to cooking

measuring cup

can opener

pot holders

tongs

large bowl

wooden spoon

measuring cup(s)

grater

knife

measuring spoons

tablespoon

teaspoon

cutting board

blender

mixer

pans

cake pan(s)

*Always ask your parents before using these recipes. Wash your hands, follow all the directions, and Always be careful!*

baking pan 9" × 13" × 3"

cookie sheet

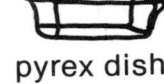

pyrex dish

**3**

# BEANS

Little Stuart the Skunk bought two kinds of green bean seeds, one packet of bush beans and one of pole beans, and with his parent's help, planted them. They chose a sunny spot in the backyard and turned over the ground with a shovel about eight inches deep and raked it smooth.

Stuart carefully read and followed all the directions that came on the back of the seed package. He waited until the ground was warm because beans can rot and die in cold or freezing soil.

He planted his bush beans about three inches apart and covered them with an inch of dirt. It was easy! He also planted four or five "pole" beans around a stake. All of Stuart's beans grew well because he watered and weeded his garden daily.

An easy way to store beans is to freeze them. Even though Stuart's parents do most of the work, he is a big help to them. He washes the beans and carefully cuts them into pieces. Mrs. Skunk puts the cut beans into a wire mesh basket and drops it into boiling water for three to five minutes. She cools the beans quickly in ice water, puts them into containers and into the freezer. The Skunks now have plenty of beans for a "rainy day"

Stuart also enjoys boiled green beans, or better yet, steamed beans for dinner. The beans steam in a basket that sits in a deep pan. Put enough water in a pan to come up to the bottom of the basket. Cover the pan tightly and bring water to a bubbling boil. Let the beans steam for 15 minutes more. The beans are tender and good!

# BEANS

*I'VE 'BEAN' WAITING FOR THIS MOMENT!*

## STEAMED GREEN BEANS & TOMATO SALAD

Ingredients: 3 tablespoons of vinegar

3 tablespoons of oil

½ teaspoon of salt

¼ teaspoon of pepper

1 teaspoon of sugar

2 cups of cooled, fresh, steamed or boiled green beans

2 large tomatoes

1 small sliced cucumber

Steps: 1. Stuart Skunk mixes the vinegar, oil, & sugar together in a deep bowl.

2. He adds the beans, tomatoes, and cucumber.

3. He can serve this salad now, or chill it first in the refrigerator and serve it later.

# BEETS

THE SUN SHINES
THE RAIN FALLS,
AND EVERY DAY
THE BEETS GROW
TALL!

7

# BEETS

Roxanne Raccoon's garden is one of the best in the neighborhood, and one of the easiest vegetables to grow in Roxanne's garden is the beet. Beets grow almost everywhere and can be planted early in the spring. Roxanne planted the seeds half an inch deep and three inches apart. Roxanne knows that beets are rich in vitamins and minerals, especially iron. She also knows that they are very tasty to eat.

When the beets are one inch in size or larger, Roxanne cuts off the roots and tops and washes them well. Then she cooks them in boiling, salted water until she can easily stick a fork into them. If the beets are very large they may have to cook for as long as sixty minutes. Roxanne peels the beets after they are cooked and cooled.

She stores uncooked beets in a big box in a cool place where they keep very well for a long time.

PICKLED BEETS

You will need:

 Pot   Cutting Board   Knife   Spoon

 Measuring Spoons   Measuring Cup   Tongs   Bowl

Ingredients:

1 cup cooked, sliced beets
1 cup beet juice
½ cup apple cider vinegar
½ teaspoon garlic powder
6 cloves

Steps:

1. Cook beets in water until tender.
2. Save the water!
3. Cool and slice.
4. Put 1 cup of cooked, sliced beets into a bowl and add 1 cup of the beet juice water you saved.
5. Add vinegar, garlic and cloves. (Onion slices are good too, you should try them!) Pickled beets should be served cold at dinner. Keep in the refrigerator.

# CARROTS

Roy Rabbit planted only one vegetable this year — carrots! He turned the ground over eight inches deep. Carrots need to grow in loose, rich dirt, free of rocks and slightly sandy. Roy planted more seeds than he thought would grow, half an inch deep. He made sure that the ground was moist, particularly for the first two or three weeks after planting. Carrots take 65 to 75 days to grow from a seed. The little carrot plants had to be thinned so the others could grow better.

THIS CARROT TASTES LIKE A WINNER TO ME!

Carrots stay fresh when stored in the vegetable bin in the refrigerator. Sometimes Roy even leaves them in the ground during the winter months although they should be covered with straw or leaves if the ground freezes.

But Roy won't have many carrots to store this year. He eats them up too fast! Nothing tastes better than a fresh, sweet carrot. Turn the page for some of Roy's best carrot recipes.

# CARROTS

I'M PROUD OF MY CARROTS.
I DID EVERYTHING JUST RIGHT!

# CARROTS

CARROT SOUP FOR TWO

You will need:

grater

measuring cup

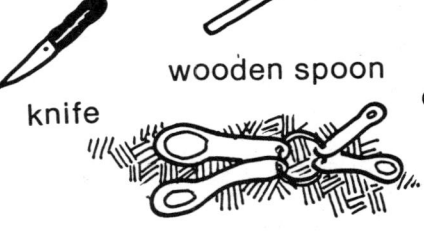

knife

wooden spoon

measuring spoons

cutting board

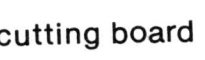

pan

Ingredients:

½ teaspoon of butter (or margarine)
2 medium carrots (grated)
1 small tomato (chopped)
1 cup of chicken broth or 1 cup or water and 2 chicken
    bouillon cubes
2 tablespoons of plain yogurt

Steps:

1. Heat the grated carrots in a saucepan with the butter (or margarine) until very tender.
2. Add the chopped tomato and half the broth and cook on medium heat for 5 minutes, stirring regularly.
3. Add the rest of the broth and simmer for 20 minutes.
4. Add the 2 tablespoons of yogurt and serve hot.
   Roy and Maynard gobble it up!

**13**

# CARROTS

## CARROT CAKE

There are lots of ingredients in this Carrot Cake Recipe for Roy to gather, but it really isn't very hard to make at all!

You will need:

 grater

large bowl    wooden spoon

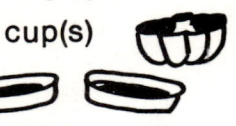 measuring spoons
measuring cup(s)

 mixer

cake pan(s)

Ingredients:

2 cups of all-purpose flour or whole wheat flour

1 cup of sugar

1 cup of brown sugar

1 teaspoon of baking powder

1 teaspoon of baking soda

1 teaspoon of salt

1 teaspoon of cinnamon

3 cups of shredded carrots (about 3 carrots)

1 cup of vegetable oil

4 eggs

Steps:

1. Combine flour, sugars, baking powder and soda, salt and cinnamon together in a bowl and mix well.
2. Grate the carrots and add to the mixture.
3. Add cooking oil and eggs. Beat with a mixer until everything is smooth and creamy. (About 2 minutes.)
4. Did you notice that Roy forgot to grease and flour the pan? This will be a good time to do that little job.
5. Pour the cake mixture into the greased pan and bake in the oven at 325° for 50-60 minutes. That's a long time. Don't get impatient like Roy does sometimes. Once he opened the oven door way too soon and the poor cake never rose any higher!

   The cake is done when you can stick a fork into it and it comes out clean.

# CARROTS

## CARROT AND POTATO PATTIES

Ingredients:

2 cups of cold mashed potatoes

1 large carrot

1 teaspoon of vegetable oil or pat of margarine or butter

Steps:

1. You will need 1 grated carrot for every 2 cups of cold, mashed potatoes.
2. Mix well and shape them into patties.
3. Fry them in a skillet with a little oil or margarine. Cook until golden brown on both sides.

## CARROT STICKS AND CHEESEY DIP

Choose four or five of the best carrots from your garden. Wash them shiny clean. Cut the tops and bottoms off. You should ask an older person to help you cut the carrots into 6" sticks. Put the carrots in ice water and store in the refrigerator until just before eating.

## PINEAPPLE CREAM CHEESE VEGETABLE DIP

Ingredients:

1 8 oz. package of cream cheese

3 tablespoons of crushed pineapple

Steps:

1. Mash the crushed pineapple into soft cream cheese. Mix it up very well in a medium-sized bowl.
2. Put the bowl on a platter and surround the carrot sticks (and other fresh, raw vegetables). Dip the carrot sticks into the mixture and give your taste buds a treat!

# CORN

Poor Susan! Every year she gets herself stuck up on a cornstalk and cannot get down! Susan climbed the cornstalk in order to test the corn for ripeness. If the kernels are milky inside, the corn is ready to harvest.

Susan and Simon planted their first corn crop early in the season when all danger of frost had passed. They planted their second crop ten days later, and a third one ten days after that. They wanted to be sure that they had plenty of corn for the winter.

Before the Squirrels planted their corn, they carefully prepared the soil. Using shovels, they turned the ground over to eight or more inches deep. They wanted it loose, moist, and free of weeds.

Simon spaced his rows thirty inches apart and put two or three seeds in each hole. The holes were about one foot apart. He watered the baby plants daily, particularly while the corn was tassling and forming ears.

Now that some of the corn is ready to be harvested, Susan and Simon will pick it, take the brown outer husks off, and store some of the corn in the refrigerator. They will eat the corn as soon as possible before the sugar turns to starch. They will save the rest by boiling it immediately for five minutes and then freezing it. Home-grown corn is the best corn in the world!!!

# CORN

### SUSAN'S TAMALE SOUP
### WITH CHEESE AND CHIPS

**You will need:**

saucepan  can opener  grater  cutting board  knife  spoon

measuring cup

**Ingredients:**

1 - 16 oz. can tomato sauce

1 - 16 oz. can stewed tomatoes

2 cups fresh cooked corn cut off the cob or

    1 - 16 oz. can whole kernel corn

1 - 2 oz. can sliced black olives

1 medium bell pepper

½ cup water

¼ - ½ cup cornmeal

1 cup grated cheddar cheese

lots of tortilla chips

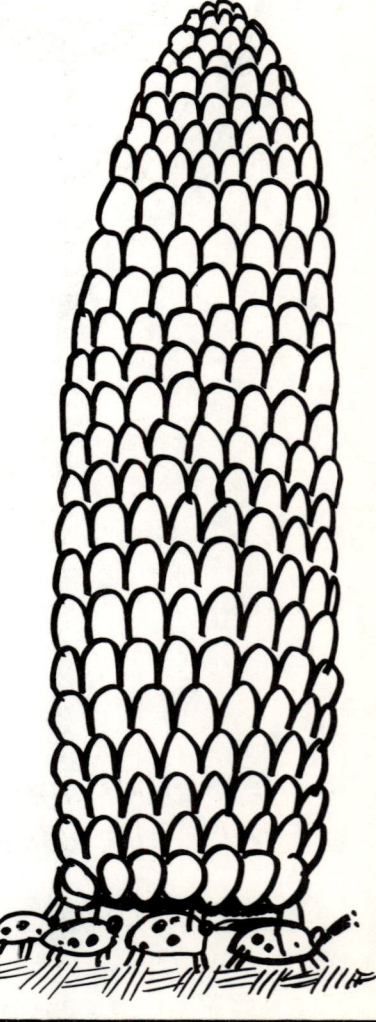

**Step:**

1. Mix and heat tomato sauce and stewed tomatoes in a saucepan.
2. Chop and add the bell pepper.
3. Add the olives and corn kernels.
4. Add ½ cup of water
5. Slowly add corn meal stirring well. Mixture should be thicker than tomato sauce but less thick than oatmeal.
6. Bring mixture to a boiling bubble.
7. When hot pour into chili bowl, garnish with grated cheese and tortilla chips. Serve to your very best friends.

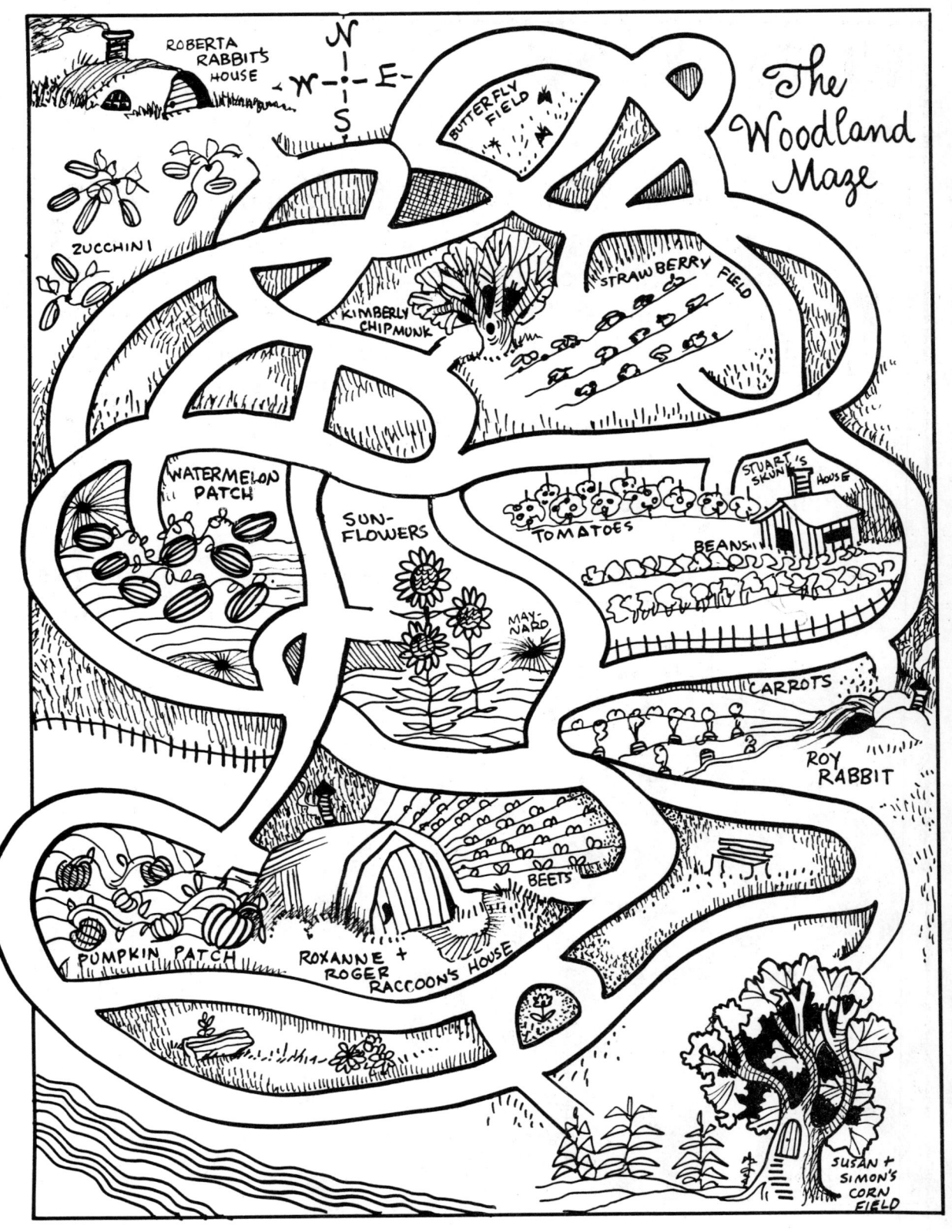

The Woodland Maze

CAN YOU FIND THE WAY FROM SUSAN SQUIRREL'S HOUSE TO ROBERTA RABBIT'S HOUSE?
HOW ABOUT FROM THE PUMPKIN PATCH TO THE STRAWBERRY FIELD?

# PUMPKINS

Roxanne Raccoon is always glad to show off her pumpkin patch to her brother, Roger. This year's crop is one of her best. She started in the spring when the days were warm and sunny. She built several small hills of dirt six feet apart and planted eight to ten seeds in each hill. When the seeds began to grow, she pulled out the weaker ones so that not more than four vines grew from each mound. She got more pumpkins from the better vines this way. She watered her pumpkins every day, just at the roots so that the water wouldn't rot the rest of the plant.

ROXANNE! THIS IS THE MOST WONDERFUL, TERRIFIC, FANTASTIC, STUPENDOUS AND AMAZING PUMPKIN PATCH I HAVE EVER SEEN!

YOU SAID IT, ROGER!

# PUMPKINS

Roxanne's pumpkins used to get brown and moldy where they lay on the ground. This year she put black plastic under each pumpkin and they grew smooth and orange all over.

Roxanne stores only the best, unbruised pumpkins. She cuts them off the vine, leaving several inches of stem, and takes them into the house for ten days. Then she moves them into a fruit cellar or shed, or garage, and lines them on the shelves. She never stacks them on top of one another.

If Roxanne doesn't have a lot of room to store her pumpkins some years, she sells them to her friends and neighbors at Halloween time for jack-o-lanterns!

I'M GLAD YOU LIKE IT! ———

# PUMPKINS

THIS IS A FEAST FIT FOR A KING!

ROASTED PUMPKIN SEEDS

Would you like to know what to do with all of those left-over pumpkin seeds?

Roger and Roxanne wash them in a strainer, put them in a bowl and mix with 2 tablespoons of cooking oil and a teaspoon of salt. (Add more oil if you have a lot of pumpkin seeds.) Then they spread them on a cookie sheet and put them into the oven (250°) for an hour and a half or so. The pumpkin seeds will be golden brown and crunchy when done.

# PUMPKINS

TRY ONE OF MY FAMOUS PUMPKIN COOKIES, YOUR HIGHNESS!

## HOW TO STEAM FRESH PUMPKIN

Steps:

1. Wash the pumpkin.
2. Pare off the outer skin and cut into cubes.
3. Steam in a wire mesh basket over boiling water for 25 minutes, or until tender.
4. Put the cooled pumpkin into a bowl and mash with a potato masher. You can store it for a couple of days in a closed container in the refrigerator, or use it to make pumpkin cookies or pumpkin bread.

# PUMPKINS

### ROGER'S PUMPKIN NUT BREAD

Roger LOVES this recipe!  He turns the oven on to 350° and greases and flours a 9" × 5" × 3" loaf pan first.

You will need:

spoon

measuring spoons

measuring cup(s)

large bowl

pan

Ingredients:

⅓ cup of margarine

¾ cup of sugar

3 eggs

1¾ cups of whole wheat flour

1 teaspoon of baking powder

½ teaspoon of baking soda

½ teaspoon of salt

1 teaspoon of each; cinnamon and nutmeg

½ teaspoon of cloves

1½ cups of steamed pumpkin (or 1½ cups canned pumpkin)

½ cup of chopped walnuts

Steps:

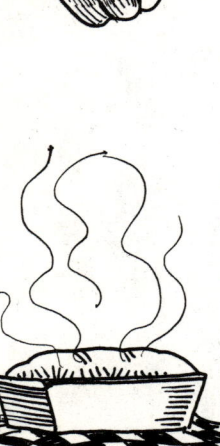

1. Cream together the sugar and margarine and eggs and beat well.
2. In a different bowl mix together the flour, baking powder and soda, salt and spices.
3. Add ½ the flour mixture and ½ the pumpkin to the creamed sugar, mix well.
4. Add the rest of the pumpkin and flour and mix very well.
5. Add the walnuts and stir.
6. Bake in the 350° oven for 45-50 minutes.
7. Cool on a wire rack.  Sometimes this kind of bread tastes better if you wrap it and let it stand over night.  Can you wait that long?  (Sometimes Roger can, and sometimes he cannot!)

# PUMPKINS

## ROXANNE RACCOON'S
## FAMOUS PUMPKIN COOKIES

Preheat the oven to 375°.

You will need:

cookie sheet

measuring spoons
measuring cup(s)

large bowl

Ingredients:

    ½ cup of margarine

    ½ cup of sugar

    ½ cup or brown sugar

    1 cup cooked or canned pumpkin

    2 eggs

    1 teaspoon vanilla

    1 teaspoon of cinnamon

    a dash of cloves and a dash of nutmeg

    (OR, ½ teaspoon of apple pie spice).

    1½ cups of flour

    ½ teaspoon of baking soda

    2 teaspoons of baking powder

    1 cup of rolled oats

Steps:

1. Mix the margarine and sugars in a bowl.
2. Add the eggs and pumpkin and vanilla, cinnamon, and spices. Mix well.
3. Stir in slowly the flour, soda, and baking powder.
4. Mix in the oats. Stir well.
5. Drop by teaspoonsful onto a greased cookie sheet. Bake 10-15 minutes.

    Pumpkin cookies are soft and chewy, plump and delicious!

# STRAWBERRIES

Kimberly Chipmunk admired Susan Squirrel's garden so much, she decided to plant one of her own. Kimberly chose strawberries for her first crop.

Strawberries need lots of water and sun so Kimberly chose a spot in her yard that is sunny all day long. In the early spring she bought 30 tiny strawberry plants from a good nursery. Kimberly and some of her Woodland friends had already prepared the soil by turning it over and mixing in a good fertilizer.

She planted the strawberries in rows, 2 or 3 feet apart with 10 plants in each row. The plants are about 12 inches away from each other in each row. Some of Kimberly's more experienced gardener friends warned her not to plant the little strawberries too deep or too shallow, but just the same as they came from the nursery. She gave each plant a good soaking after planting. And she made sure to water well every day and twice on very hot days!

Kimberly discovered that weeds were a big problem in her strawberry patch. She had to pick them and hoe regularly. She also had some trouble from birds who picked at the pink and attractive fruit. Kimberly finally had to buy nylon anti-bird netting at the nursery and lay it over the plants for protection.

Once her plants began producing berries, Kimberly picked the ripe ones every day.

In late fall, Kimberly mulched her strawberry patch for winter. Mulching means that she placed a 2 inch thick layer of straw over her plants to protect them from freezing. She will get good harvest from her plants for 2 or 3 years if she protects them in the winter. Bales of straw can be purchased at a nursery or Grange.

# STRAWBERRIES

STRAWBERRIES ARE, WITHOUT A DOUBT, THE SWEETEST- SMELLING PLANTS THAT GROW!

# STRAWBERRY

## SOME OF THE MANY USES FOR STRAWBERRIES

1. Wash and eat right away — fresh off the vine!

2. Wash and remove stems and freeze in a proper container for eating next week — or, next month!

3. Wash and remove stems, slice in half and mix in a bowl with 1 teaspoon of powdered sugar. Spoon over vanilla ice cream.

4. Mix fresh strawberries with strawberry gelatin and set. (Overnight is best.) Serve to your family and friends with whipped topping and more fresh strawberries.

5. Make your own Strawberry Topping for pancakes and waffles. Wash, cut and stem and mash strawberries in a blender or by hand. Add 1 teaspoon of sugar for each cup of mashed berries. Pour over hot pancakes or waffles.

6. Make your own Strawberry Tea! Cover a cupful of washed strawberry leaves with 4 cups of boiling hot water. Cover and let steep for 5 minutes. Add a teaspoon of honey if desired, and enjoy your fragrant tea.

7. Last — but not least. Throw some washed strawberry leaves into your next green salad! The unique flavor is very delightful and tastes especially good with one of the creamy dressings like Stuart's Easy Thousand Island Dressing on page 39.

# STRAWBERRY

## STRAWBERRY-BANANA YOGURT SHAKE

You will need:

knife

cutting board

blender

Glasses

Ingredients:

    1 cup frozen unsweetened strawberries
    2 small ripe bananas
    2 cups of plain unsweetened yogurt
    ½ teaspoon of vanilla

Steps:

1. In a blender combine the yogurt, sliced bananas and vanilla. Blend until creamy.
2. Slowly add the strawberries a few at a time. Blend until smooth.
3. Pour into glasses and drink, or, chill first, or, pour into small cups and freeze. Eat it like soft ice cream!

# SUNFLOWERS

IT CERTAINLY WAS A
LUCKY DAY WHEN I
PLANTED THOSE
SUNFLOWER SEEDS!

# SUNFLOWERS

Some of the sunflowers that Maynard the Mouse planted are fifteen feet tall!  Everyone in the neighborhood admires their height and beauty.  Would you believe that Maynard had never planted anything before in his life?

His sunflowers were easy to grow.  He chose a sunny spot and watered every day to keep them standing straight and tall.

Maynard cut down the sunflowers when the seeds took on a brownish tinge.  He cut and hung the flower heads upside-down in a warm, dry place.  When the seeds are dry they can be roasted and eaten.  Maynard soaks them overnight in salt water, drains them and spreads the seeds on a cookie sheet.  He roasts them in a warm oven (250°) for three or more hours.  Then he shells and eats them!  He saves some in a jar for using in salads or eating as a snack.

### MAYNARD'S NUTTY SANDWICH SPREAD

knife
cutting board
large bowl  grater

wooden spoon
measuring spoons
measuring cup

Ingredients:

1 cup of dry roasted sunflower seeds shelled (or soy nuts, or peanuts ) chopped fine    ¼ teaspoon of salt

1 medium carrot grated

2 tablespoons of raisins

¼ cup of mayonnaise

4 tablespoons of honey

4 pieces of bread or rolls, your choice

Steps:

1.  Mix the ingredients in a bowl.
2.  Spread it on bread and eat it.

# TOMATOES

Stuart the Skunk decided to plant tomatoes as well as green beans in his garden this year. He bought a dozen baby tomato plants at the nursery and kept them indoors until the frosty weather was gone.

He then planted the little plants in full sunlight. Stuart's dad or mom had already tilled the ground about a foot deep and had mixed fertilizer into the dirt. Stuart carefully set his plants into little holes three feet apart and watered them well at the roots.

As the tomato bushes began to grow, Stuart worried about letting them trail along the ground. His father explained that he could tie his bushy tomato plants up onto stakes or prop them up with circles of chicken wire.

If you thought Stuart had a lot of green beans, you should see his tomatoes! He has given baskets of fresh tomatoes away to his friends and relatives. It's nice to be able to share the harvest from your very own garden.

# TOMATOES

TOMATOES ARE RED,
THE SKY IS BLUE.
I'M A HAPPY SKUNK,
HOPE YOU ARE, TOO!

# TOMATOES

## FRESH TOMATO JUICE

1. In a blender, juice 3 cups of chopped tomatoes, 3 tablespoons of lemon juice, 1 teaspoon of Worchestershire sauce, ½ teaspoon of salt, ½ teaspoon of celery seasoning and a dash of pepper.

2. Keep your tomato juice in the refrigerator until ready to use.

WORCHESTERSHIRE SAUCE

# TOMATOES

### GARDEN FRESH TOMATO SALAD

Start with a crisp head of lettuce and wash in cold water. Pull the leaves off gently and place in a large bowl.

Slice firm, red tomatoes and add to the lettuce in the bowl. Add some or all of your favorite fresh, raw vegetables: cucumbers, bell peppers, broccoli, cauliflower, radishes, green beans, or even garbonzo beans.

### STUART'S EASY
### THOUSAND ISLAND DRESSING

Ingredients:

3 tablespoons of mayonnaise
1 tablespoon of catsup
½ teaspoon of vinegar
one shake of garlic powder
one shake of salt

Steps:

1. Put the mayonnaise in a bowl and then add the catsup.
2. Mix until the mayo is a nice light pink color with no lumps.
3. Add the other ingredients and mix again.
   The whole family will love your "easy" salad dressing!

35

# WATERMELON

# WATERMELON

Maynard Mouse has cousins who have a watermelon patch. And it looks as if Maynard is just in time for a watermelon picnic.

Once the earth was plowed for them by their good friend, Bruce the Farm Horse, the mice had no trouble at all in growing fine big watermelons.

Watermelons prefer to grow in warm, sunny climates, but there are several midget varieties that need much less room and do not mind the cooler areas.

The mice planted six or more seeds to a hole, six feet apart in any direction. Later, they thinned out the plants to one strong vine per hole. This lets the watermelon grow big and healthy.

Watermelon is healthy, too! It has many vitamins and minerals, especially vitamin C. And it is much lower in calories than many think. Half an inch of watermelon has only half the calories of a medium-sized apple!

When watermelon is ripe, it gives off a dull thud when rapped with a finger. That is the time to invite all the mice over for a watermelon picnic!

HOLD IT COUSINS! SAVE SOME FOR ME!

ME, TOO!

# ZUCCHINI

Zucchini is a summer squash. As a matter of fact, it is a relative of the pumpkin.

Roberta Rabbit, who is a mother, knows that zucchini is a very important vegetable and that it will keep her babies strong and healthy.

Zucchini is very easy to grow. Roberta planted hers in rows four feet apart. She sometimes plants them in little hills similar to those in Roxanne Raccoon's pumpkin patch. The hills should be six feet apart. Zucchini likes a lot of room in which to spread out. Like pumpkins, it can be grown on plastic to protect it from the moist earth.

Roberta stores some of her zucchini the same as pumpkins, but some of it she freezes. She washes and cuts it into two-inch thick pieces, puts the pieces in a wire basket and sets the basket in boiling water for three minutes. She chills the squash quickly by dunking it in ice water. Then she puts the zucchini into plastic bags or containers and freezes.

Roberta's little babies think that they do not like zucchini, but they are in for a surprise!

I HATE ZUCCHINI !

ME, TOO !!

IT'S YUCKY !!!

# ZUCCHINI

# ZUCCHINI

## EASY ZUCCHINI SPAGHETTI SAUCE

You will need:

Saucepan      Pot      cutting board      knife
         measuring spoons              can opener

Ingredients:

1 medium or small zucchini, cut into ¼-inch round pieces

1 11 oz. can of tomato sauce

¼ teaspoon of salt

¼ teaspoon of pepper

¼ teaspoon of oregano

1. Mix ingredients in a small sauce pan and simmer until zucchini is soft.

2. Pour the sauce over cooked spaghetti, macaroni, or pasta shells.

Steps:

1. Mix ingredients in a small sauce pan and simmer until zucchini is soft.

2. Pour the sauce over cooked spaghetti, macaroni, or pasta shells.

Baby rabbits like this recipe because it is not too spicy and it makes the zucchini taste so good!

## ZUCCHINI BARS WITH CHOCOLATE CHIPS

**You will need:**

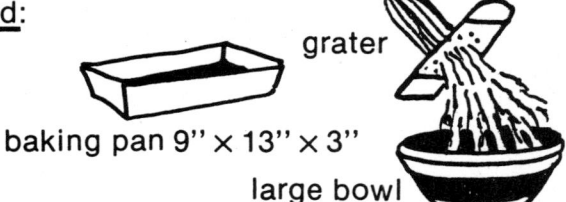

baking pan 9" × 13" × 3"     grater     large bowl     measuring cup(s)

**Ingredients:**

½ cup of brown sugar

2 eggs

¾ cup of soft margarine

1 teaspoon vanilla

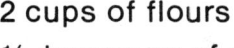

2 cups of flours

½ teaspoon of salt

½ teaspoon of baking powder

1¼ cups of raw, grated zucchini (do not peel)

¾ cup of chocolate chips

**Steps:**

1. Mix margarine, sugar, eggs and vanilla.
2. Add the flour, salt and baking powder.  Mix again
3. Add the zucchini and the chocolate chips.
4. Spread on a greased pan and bake at 350° for 30-35 minutes.
5. Clean up.
   (Thank you!)
6. Don't eat all the zucchini bars.  Save some for your mother.

YOU KNOW, THIS STUFF IS PRETTY GOOD!

# 29 Words to grow on!

| | |
|---|---|
| ear | rows |
| harvest | straw |
| tea | crop |
| rototiller | compost |
| shovel | sod |
| tassel | two |
| leaves | rules |
| loose | dip |
| stems | rid |
| roots | arid |
| plow | husk |
| hoe | weed |
| freeze | till |
| cold | hay |
| pea | |

```
H Y A H I E Z E E R F
A C E C H A E P R A E
R O T O T I L L E R R
V M E L A S O O O O T
E P L D S E O W Q O I
S O E K S V S M E T S
T S V S E A E P D S P
P T O U L E X I O Y O
I W H H U L R D E R R
D O S T R A W E E D C
```

# Measure Up   A COOKING CROSSWORD

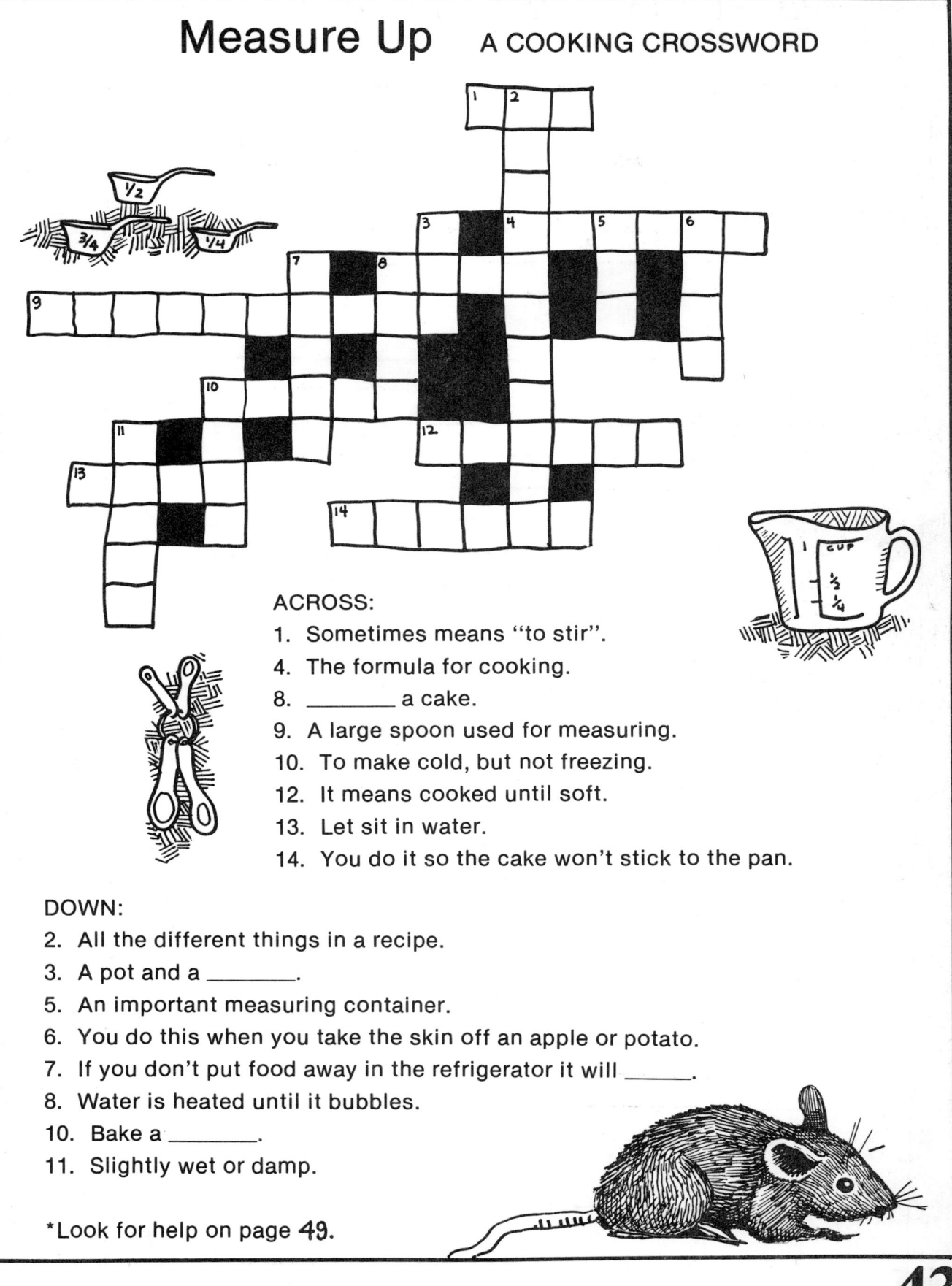

ACROSS:

1. Sometimes means "to stir".
4. The formula for cooking.
8. _____ a cake.
9. A large spoon used for measuring.
10. To make cold, but not freezing.
12. It means cooked until soft.
13. Let sit in water.
14. You do it so the cake won't stick to the pan.

DOWN:

2. All the different things in a recipe.
3. A pot and a _____.
5. An important measuring container.
6. You do this when you take the skin off an apple or potato.
7. If you don't put food away in the refrigerator it will _____.
8. Water is heated until it bubbles.
10. Bake a _____.
11. Slightly wet or damp.

*Look for help on page 49.

43

# Use this Page to Write Your Favorite Recipes:

recipe for: _____

ingredients: ___ ____ _____ ____
___ ____ _____ ____

Steps:
_____
_____
_____
_____
_____
_____
_____

recipe for: _____

ingredients: ___ ____ _____ ____
___ ____ _____ ____

Steps:
_____
_____
_____
_____
_____
_____

## Use this Page to Write Your Favorite Recipes:

recipe for: _____

ingredients: _____ _____ _____
_____ _____ _____
_____ _____ _____

Steps: _____
_____
_____
_____
_____
_____
_____

recipe for: _____

ingredients: _____ _____ _____
_____ _____ _____

Steps: _____
_____
_____
_____
_____
_____
_____

"I'm
A Good Gardener"
Award

Presented to:

for dedication and diligence; for watering and
weeding; for never giving up; and for growing
the most wonderful garden EVER !

Roxanne and Roger Raccoon
Chairmen of the Woodland Forest
Little Growers Assoc.

date:

# "I'm A Good Cook!"

for reading and following ALL directions;
for practicing Safety Habits in the kitchen;
and for always cleaning up the mess—
this Certificate of Merit is Awarded to

_____

date: _____

signatures of Roxanne and
Roger Raccoon

# a child's guide to gardening

## DICTIONARY OF PLANTING WORDS

**cellar** - a cool place, usually underground, used to store vegetables.

**climate** - the kind of weather and rainfall usual to an area.

**compost** - a fertiziling mixture of decomposed vegetable matter.

**crop** - what you have grown in your garden is your crop.

**fertilizer** - manure or nitrates used to enrich the soil.

**freeze** - the damage caused when the ground becomes stiff and icy in winter. Freezing can kill some plants.

**harvest** - gathering or collecting ripe fruit and vegetables.

**hoe** - a tool for weeding with a flat blade and long handle.

**husk** - outer coating on some vegetables, fruits and seeds. Corn husk is a good example.

**leaves** - decomping leaves make a good compost.

**manure** - animal dung or other compost added to soil.

**moist** - slightly wet or damp.

**mulch** - loose material like straw and leaves placed around stalks to protect roots from freezing.

**nursery** - a place where plants are raised for sale.

**plow** - turning over the soil very deeply.

**produce** - in gardening, a word for all your harvested vegetables.

**ripe** - grown until fit to eat.

**roots** - the underground part of a plant that absorbs moisture and food through the soil.

**rototiller** - a machine that tills the soil.

**rows** - arranged in a line.

**shallow** - in planting, not deep.

**shovel** - a flat scoop with a long handle for digging.

**stake** - a stick or post driven into the ground which some plants use as an anchor as they grow up.

**stems** - the main stalk of a plant, or the slender part that supports the flower or fruit.

**store** - put away for future use.

**straw** - a good mulch

**tassel** - the loose, silky threads on the end of the corn ears.

**to thin** - to remove the dead or weak plants so the others grow stronger.

**till** - to dig and turn the soil for the better growth of plants and seeds.

## DICTIONARY OF COOKING TERMS

**bake** - to cook inside an oven.

**blend** - to mix up and make smooth.

**boil** - when water or liquids are heated until gas escapes in bubbles.

**chill** - a certain degree of coldness, as in a refrigerator, but not freezing.

**crush** - to press or squeeze out of shape.

**cup** - a measure equal to 8 oz. or half pint.

**dash** - a very small amount, one shake of salt might be a 'dash'.

**drain** - to remove water slowly, to pour off liquid carefully.

**freeze** - to become hard and stiff with ice - as food does in a 'freezer'.

**fry** - to cook in hot fat in a skillet over an open fire.

**grate** - to rub or grind vegetables or cheese against a sharp surface making
   a crumbly mixture or powder.

**grease** - to smear a pot or pan with fat or margarine to avoid sticking.

**ingredients** - all the things together that make a recipe.

**mash** - the same as crush.

**mix** - to make something, as a cake, by combining all the ingredients.
   Also means to <u>stir.</u>

**pare** - to trim or grate away the outer skin or coverings.

**preheat** - to warm up the oven 5-10 minutes before using.

**recipe** - a formula giving proper directions for mixing ingredients in
   cooking.

**roast** - to cook slowly in the oven.

**simmer** - a frying pan with a long handle.

**skillet** - a frying pan with a long handle.

**simmer** - to boil gently.

**slice** - thin pieces cut off a larger piece.

**soak** - leaving in water until completely wet through and through.

**steam** - is just water vapor. Hot vapor rises through the steaming vegetables and cooks them.

**strainer** - a container with small holes through which excess water drains.

**tablespoon** - a fairly large spoon used for measuring.

**teaspoon** - a small measuring spoon.

**tender** - in cooking - when the vegetables are cooked soft enough for a
   knife or fork to be inserted.

Answers

page 43.

page 42.

```
HYAHIEZEERF
ACECHAEPRAE
ROTOTILLERR
VMELASOOOOT
EPLDSEOWQOI
SOEKSVSMETS
TSVSEAEPDSP
PTOULEXIOYO
IWHHULRDERR
DOSTRAWEEDC
```

the end